mapping

ASIA

Gareth Stevens
Publishing

By Barbara Linde

Please visit our website, www.garethstevens.com. For a free color catalog of all our high-quality books, call toll free 1-800-542-2595 or fax 1-877-542-2596.

Library of Congress Cataloging-in-Publication Data

Linde, Barbara M.
 Mapping Asia / Barbara M. Linde.
     pages cm. — (Mapping the world)
 Includes index.
 ISBN 978-1-4339-9100-4 (pbk.)
 ISBN 978-1-4339-9101-1 (6-pack)
 ISBN 978-1-4339-9099-1 (library binding)
 1. Maps—Asia—Juvenile literature. 2. Cartography—Asia—Juvenile literature. I. Title.
 GA1081.L48 2014
 915—dc23

                         2012049123

First Edition

Published in 2014 by
Gareth Stevens Publishing
111 East 14th Street, Suite 349
New York, NY 10003

Designer: Katelyn E. Reynolds
Editor: Kristen Rajczak

Photo credits: Cover, p. 1 (photo) Jun Baby/Shutterstock.com; cover, pp. 1, 5 (map) Uwe Dedering/Wikipedia.com; cover, pp. 1–24 (banner) kanate/Shutterstock.com; cover, pp. 1–24 (series elements and cork background) iStockphoto/Thinkstock.com; p. 7 charobnica/Shutterstock.com; p. 9 The World Factbook/CIA; p. 11 (inset) Steve Allen/Brand X Pictures/Thinkstock.com; p. 11 (main) AridOcean/Shutterstock.com; p. 13 (both) Arne Hückelheim/Wikipedia.com; pp. 15 (inset), 19 (main) iStockphoto/Thinkstock.com; p. 15 (main) TPG/Getty Images; p. 17 (inset) Ed Jones/AFP/Getty Images; p. 17 (main) Miguel Contreras, Guatemala/Wikipedia.com; p. 19 (inset) Lonely Planet Images/Getty Images; p. 20 (sketch) Ohmega1982/Shutterstock.com; p. 21 (flag pins) Vjom/Shutterstock.com; p. 21 (flags and map) ekler/Shutterstock.com.

Printed in the United States of America

CPSIA compliance information: Batch #CS13GS: For further information contact Gareth Stevens, New York, New York at 1-800-542-2595.

CONTENTS

Welcome to Asia 4

Where Is Asia? 6

The Countries of Asia 8

The Landforms of Asia 10

The Climates of Asia 12

The Resources of Asia 14

The Population of Asia 16

The Cities of Asia 18

The Landmarks of Asia 20

Glossary 22

For More Information 23

Index 24

Words in the glossary appear in **bold** type the first time they are used in the text.

WELCOME TO ASIA

Asia is the largest of the seven **continents**. It's about 17.2 million square miles (45 million sq km). That's one-third of the land on Earth!

Look at the map on the next page to see Asia's borders. The Arctic Ocean lies to the north. The Pacific Ocean lies to the east. The Indian Ocean lies to the south. Another continent, Europe, forms part of the western border. Smaller bodies of water form the rest of the western border.

Where in the World?

Together, the continents of Asia and Europe are called Eurasia. Eurasia is the largest body of land on Earth. The unofficial border between the two continents is the Ural Mountains.

4

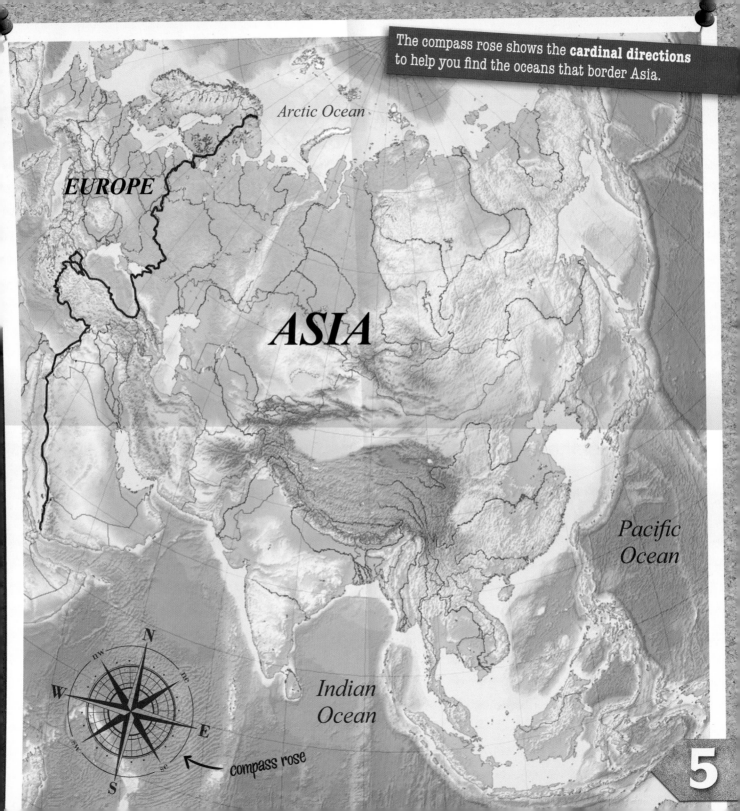

Arctic Ocean

EUROPE

ASIA

Pacific Ocean

Indian Ocean

N
nw   ne
W   E
sw   se
S

compass rose

WHERE IS ASIA?

The equator is an imaginary line around the middle of Earth. It helps us describe where places are on a map. Most of Asia is north of the equator, so we say it's in the Northern **Hemisphere**. Asia's land that falls below the equator is in the Southern Hemisphere.

Another imaginary line helps us find places on the globe. It's called the Prime Meridian, and it divides Earth into Eastern and Western Hemispheres. Asia is in the Eastern Hemisphere.

Where in the World?

Because it's so large, Asia is often divided into six parts, or regions. They're north, central, southwest (sometimes called west), south, southeast, and east Asia.

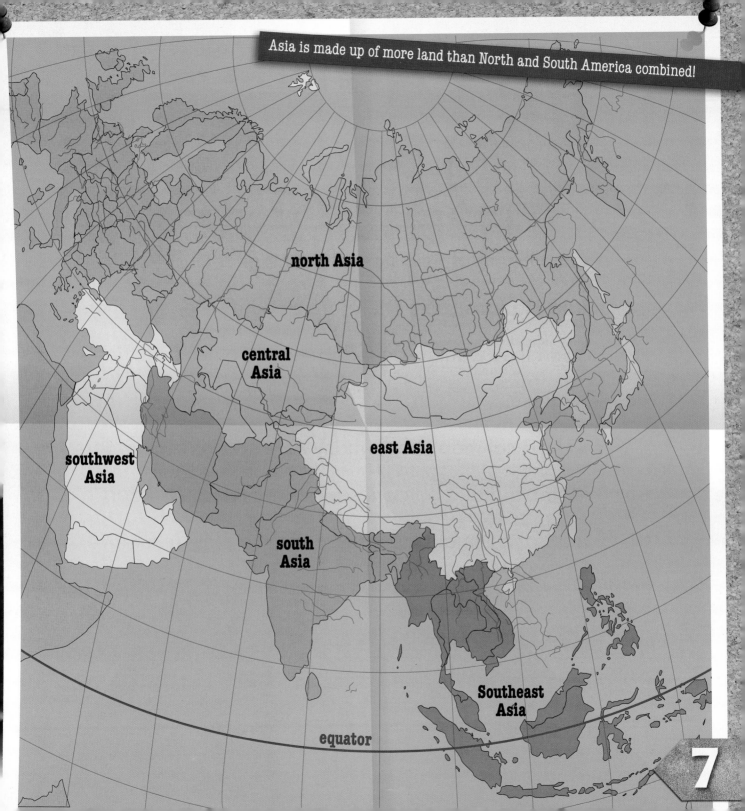

north Asia

central Asia

southwest Asia

east Asia

south Asia

Southeast Asia

equator

THE COUNTRIES OF ASIA

The continent of Asia has 48 countries recognized by the **United Nations** (UN). There are about five or six others, too. Though they want to be independent, other countries still claim them.

This political map shows many Asian countries' borders. China is so big that it borders several nations. Its border with India is the Himalayas. Rivers, including the Amur River, create the Chinese-Russian border.

Indonesia, Japan, and the Philippines are islands. The Pacific Ocean separates them from the rest of Asia.

8

Where in the World?

Sometimes, a country's borders may change. It may add land from another country or divide into more than one country. Taiwan used to be part of China, but now it's trying to claim independence.

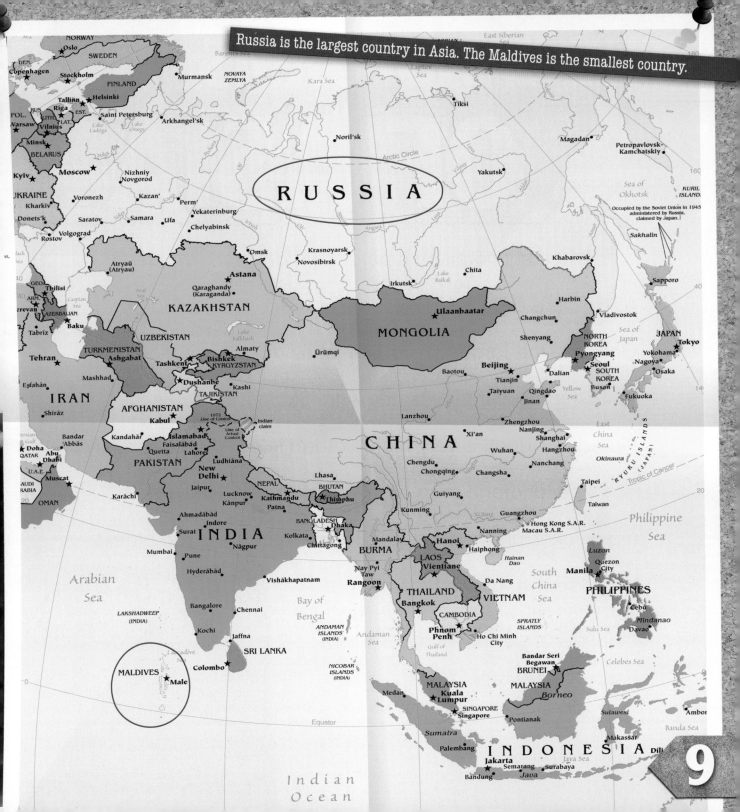

NORWAY
Oslo
SWEDEN
DEN.
Copenhagen
Stockholm
FINLAND
Murmansk
Tallinn
Helsinki
POL.
Warsaw
RUS.
Riga
LAT.
EST.
Saint Petersburg
Arkhangel'sk
Minsk
Vilnius
Moscow
Nizhniy
Novgorod
Kazan'
BELARUS
Kyiv
UKRAINE
Voronezh
Perm'
Yekaterinburg
Kharkiv
Saratov
Samara
Ufa
Donets'k
Volgograd
Chelyabinsk
Rostov
Omsk
GEO.
Tbilisi
ARM.
Yerevan
AZERBAIJAN
Baku
Tabriz
Atyraū
(Atyrau)
Astana
Qaraghandy
(Karaganda)
KAZAKHSTAN
UZBEKISTAN
TURKMENISTAN
Ashgabat
Tehran
Mashhad
Tashkent
Bishkek
KYRGYZSTAN
Eşfahān
IRAN
Shīrāz
AFGHANISTAN
Kabul
Dushanbe
TAJIKISTAN
Kashi
Ürümqi
Bandar
'Abbas
Kandahār
Islamabad
Faisalābād
Quetta
Lahore
Line of
Control
Line of
Actual
Control
Indian
claim

RUSSIA

Noril'sk
Krasnoyarsk
Novosibirsk
Irkutsk
Lake
Baikal
Chita
Yakutsk
MONGOLIA
Ulaanbaatar
Tiksi
Magadan
Petropavlovsk-
Kamchatskiy
Sakhalin
Khabarovsk
Harbin
Changchun
Shenyang
NORTH
KOREA
Pyongyang
Vladivostok
Sapporo
JAPAN
Tokyo
Yokohama
Nagoya
Seoul
SOUTH
KOREA
Busan
Osaka
Fukuoka

Occupied by the Soviet Union in 1945
administered by Russia,
claimed by Japan.

Almaty
Lake
Balkhash
PAKISTAN
New
Delhi
Ludhiāna
Jaipur
NEPAL
Kathmandu
Thimphu
BHUTAN
Lucknow
Kānpur
Patna
Ahmadābād
Indore
Nāgpur
Surat
INDIA
Kolkata
BANGLADESH
Dhaka
Chittagong
Mumbai
Pune
Hyderābād
Vishākhapatnam
Bangalore
Chennai
Kochi
Jaffna
SRI LANKA
Colombo
MALDIVES
Male
Karāchi
LAKSHADWEEP
(INDIA)

Baotou
Beijing
Tianjin
Dalian
Taiyuan
Qingdao
Jinan
Lanzhou
Zhengzhou
Xi'an
Nanjing
Shanghai
Hangzhou
CHINA
Chengdu
Chongqing
Wuhan
Nanchang
Changsha
Lhasa
Guiyang
Kunming
Nanning
Guangzhou
Hong Kong S.A.R.
Macau S.A.R.
Mandalay
Hanoi
Haiphong
BURMA
Nay Pyi
Taw
Rangoon
LAOS
Vientiane
Da Nang
Hainan
Dao
THAILAND
Bangkok
VIETNAM
CAMBODIA
Phnom
Penh
Ho Chi Minh
City
MALAYSIA
Kuala
Lumpur
SINGAPORE
Singapore
Medan
Pontianak
Sumatra
Palembang
INDONESIA
Jakarta
Semarang
Surabaya
Bandung
Java

Taipei
Taiwan
Okinawa
RYUKU ISLANDS
(JAPAN)
Tropic of Cancer
Luzon
Quezon
City
Manila
PHILIPPINES
Cebú
Mindanao
Davao
SPRATLY
ISLANDS
Sulu Sea
Celebes Sea
Bandar Seri
Begawan
BRUNEI
MALAYSIA
Borneo
Sulawesi
Makassar
Ambor
Banda Sea
Dili

Sea of
Okhotsk
KURIL
ISLANDS
Sea of
Japan
Yellow
Sea
East
China
Sea
Philippine
Sea
South
China
Sea

East Siberian
Sea
Laptev
Sea
Kara Sea
Barents Sea
NOVAYA
ZEMLYA
Arctic Circle

Black
Sea
Caspian
Sea
Aral
Sea
Persian
Gulf
QATAR
Doha
Abu
Dhabi
U.A.E.
Muscat
OMAN
SAUDI
ARABIA
Arabian
Sea

Lakshadweep
Sea
Laccadive
Sea
Bay of
Bengal
ANDAMAN
ISLANDS
(INDIA)
Andaman
Sea
Gulf of
Thailand
NICOBAR
ISLANDS
(INDIA)

Indian
Ocean
Equator

9

THE LANDFORMS OF ASIA

You can find every type of landform somewhere in Asia. There are six big deserts, of which the Arabian and Gobi are the largest. Asia has many mountain ranges, including the Himalayas and Altai Shan. It also has the Plateau of Tibet, a very high plateau in southwestern China.

The landform map on the next page shows Asia's many lakes and rivers. Lake Baikal in Russia is the oldest and deepest lake in the world. It holds about 20 percent of Earth's freshwater.

Where in the World?

Mount Everest, in the Himalayas, is about 29,035 feet (8,850 m) high. It's the highest mountain the world.

This landform map shows many geographic features of Asia, including the Yangtze River. It flows for more than 3,900 miles (6,275 km) across China and is the longest river in Asia.

Lake Baikal

Gobi Desert

Altai Shan

Plateau of Tibet

Yangtze River

Arabian Desert

Himalayas

Himalayas and Mount Everest

THE CLIMATES OF ASIA

If you travel through Asia, you'll experience many different **climates**. Much of the climate differences on the continent have to do with changes in **elevation** and nearness to the ocean.

Siberia, in northern Russia, has a cold, **arid** climate. Borneo is right on the equator. Its tropical climate is hot and rainy. Much of Asia deals with monsoons, or a change in the direction of the major winds. Cold winds commonly bring cool, dry winters. Warm winds make the summers hot and rainy.

Where in the World?

Malaysia, Borneo, Sumatra, and other countries in Southeast Asia are home to some of the oldest rainforests in the world.

Monsoons have a great effect on the landscape of some parts of Asia. The photographs below of the Western Ghats in India were taken only 3 months apart!

dry season (May)

rainy season (August)

13

THE RESOURCES OF ASIA

Asia has plenty of important **natural resources**. Coal, tin, and iron are a few of the useful **minerals** found there. Western Asia has large amounts of oil. Gold is found in Siberia, North and South Korea, and a few other countries.

One of Asia's more important resources is water. The many rivers and lakes provide plenty of water for drinking. But water often has to be brought to dry areas to grow crops. Waterpower is often used to make electricity, too.

Where in the World?

Bamboo is a tall, fast-growing grass. People eat the young plants and seeds. Animals eat the leaves. Older, taller stems are used to build houses and boats.

Dams, like the Three Gorges Dam on the Yangtze River, help Asian countries make electricity and control their water resources.

bamboo hut

THE POPULATION OF ASIA

About 4 billion people live in Asia. That's more than half of the world's population! The population map on the next page shows that most of the people in Asia live in eastern China, India, and western Asia.

China alone has more than 1.3 billion people. That's the largest population of any country in the world. Even so, most families have just one child. Families in other east Asian countries are also small. Saudi Arabia and other countries in western Asia often have large families.

Where in the World?

The Maldives has the smallest population in Asia with about 320,000 people.

0–10
10–25
25–50
50–75
75–100
100–150
150–300
300–1000
1000+

*people per km²

A Chinese family
welcomes its only child.

17

THE CITIES OF ASIA

Two of the largest cities of the world are in Asian countries. The big black boxes on the map show where these cities are. Tokyo is Japan's capital. Over 13 million people live there. Most live in small apartments. Seoul, South Korea, is home to about a quarter of the population of Korea. But the city takes up less than 1 percent of the country's land!

Some of the other large cities are Mumbai, India; Shanghai, China; and Jakarta, Indonesia.

Where in the World?

The location of present-day Jakarta was first settled around the 5th century AD. In the past, it has been run by the Dutch and, briefly, the British.

A city street map, like the one of Seoul below, shows details like streets and buildings. **Tourists** use street maps to find their way in unfamiliar places.

Seoul street map

THE LANDMARKS OF ASIA

Every country has special places called landmarks. Visiting landmarks can help you learn about the people and **culture** of a country.

Some of the most famous landmarks in the world are in Asia. The Great Wall of China was built to keep enemies out of the country. An emperor built the Taj Mahal in India. He wanted to honor his wife after she died. For a super view of Dubai in the United Arab Emirates, go to the top of the Burj Khalifa skyscraper. It's the tallest building in the world!

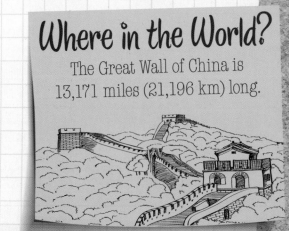

Where in the World?
The Great Wall of China is 13,171 miles (21,196 km) long.

Flags of Asia

Armenia

India

Cambodia

Japan

China

Philippines

GLOSSARY

arid: dry

cardinal directions: the main directions—north, south, east, and west

climate: the average weather conditions of a place over a period of time

continent: one of the seven large landmasses on Earth. They are Asia, Africa, Europe, North America, South America, Australia, and Antarctica.

culture: the beliefs and ways of life of a group of people

elevation: height above sea level

hemisphere: one half of Earth

mineral: matter in the ground that forms rocks

natural resource: something in nature that can be used by people

tourist: person traveling to visit another place

United Nations: a group of nations that united after World War II with the goal of solving conflicts between nations

FOR MORE INFORMATION

Books

Hirsch, Rebecca. *Asia*. New York, NY: Children's Press, 2012.

Schaefer, A. R. *Spotlight on Asia*. Mankato, MN: Capstone Press, 2011.

Websites

Asia

travel.nationalgeographic.com/travel/continents/asia/

Use this website to watch videos, read articles, and look at photographs about the continent of Asia and its many countries.

Asia: Geography

www.ducksters.com/geography/asia.php

Read facts about the geography and countries of Asia. Look at maps of each country.

Asia Society: Cool Websites for Kids

asiasociety.org/education/resources-schools/partnership-ideas/cool-websites-kids

Use this website to find links to more information about the geography, history, and culture of Asia.

INDEX

Altai Shan 10, 11

Arabian Desert 10, 11

Arctic Ocean 4, 5

Borneo 12

Burj Khalifa skyscraper 20

China 8, 10, 11, 16, 18, 20, 21

cities 18

climates 12, 17

compass rose 5

continents 4, 8, 12

countries 8, 9, 14, 15, 16, 20

equator 6, 7, 12

Europe 4, 5

flags 21

Gobi Desert 10, 11

Great Wall 20

hemispheres 6

Himalayas 8, 10, 11

India 8, 13, 16, 18, 20, 21

Indian Ocean 4, 5

Indonesia 8, 18

Japan 8, 18, 21

Lake Baikal 10, 11

landform map 10, 11

landmarks 20

Maldives 9, 16

monsoons 12, 13

Mount Everest 10, 11

natural resources 14

North Korea 14

Pacific Ocean 4, 5, 8

Philippines 8, 21

Plateau of Tibet 10, 11

political map 8, 9

population map 16, 17

Prime Meridian 6

regions 6, 7

Russia 8, 9, 10, 12

Saudi Arabia 16

Seoul 18, 19

Siberia 12, 14

South Korea 14, 18

Taj Mahal 20

Three Gorges Dam 15

Tokyo 18

United Arab Emirates 20

water 4, 10, 14, 15

Yangtze River 11, 15